Intermediate (UK Exam Grades 3–4)

THE NORTHERN PRA

Melody Bober

Prairie Stomp

Minnesota Morning

Blizzard

ISBN-10: 0-7390-5089-3
ISBN-13: 978-0-7390-5089-7

Dedicated to Music Southwest—southwest Minnesota piano teachers on the Prairie!

Prairie Stomp
SECONDO

Melody Bober

Dedicated to Music Southwest—southwest Minnesota piano teachers on the Prairie!

Prairie Stomp
PRIMO

Melody Bober

Spirited (♩ = 88–92)

Both hands one octave higher than written throughout

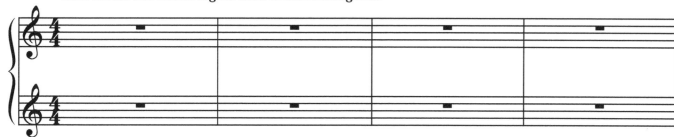

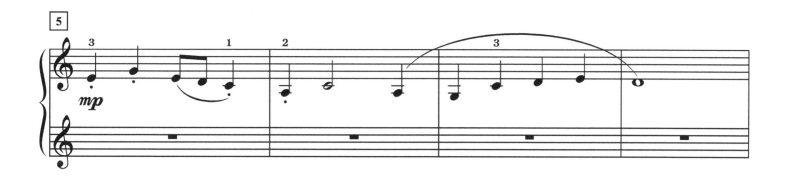

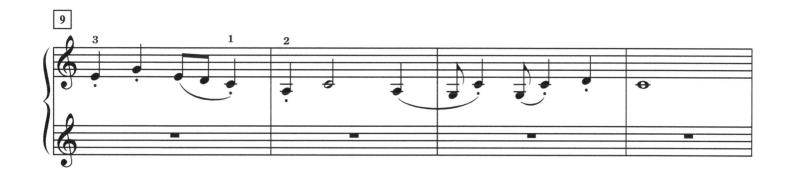

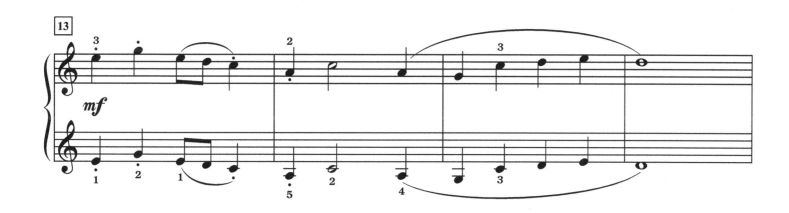

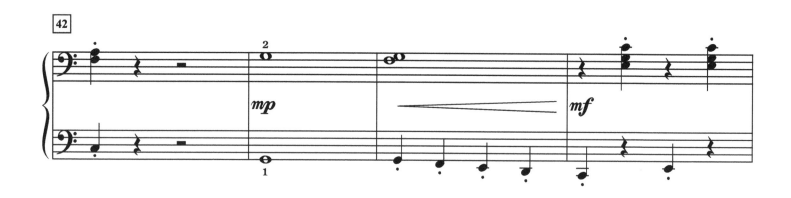

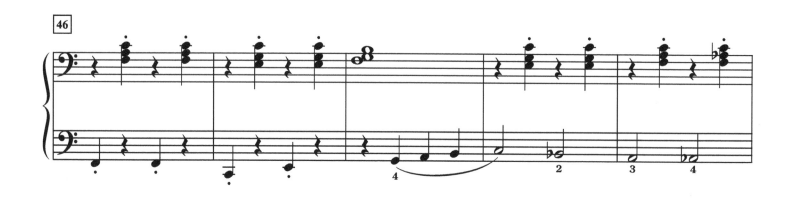

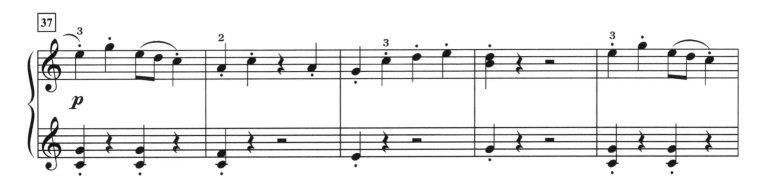

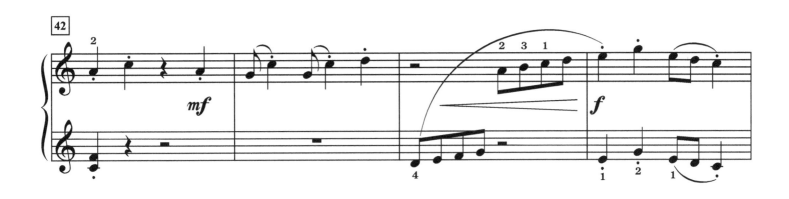

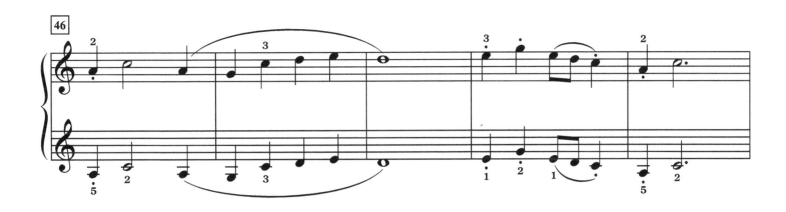

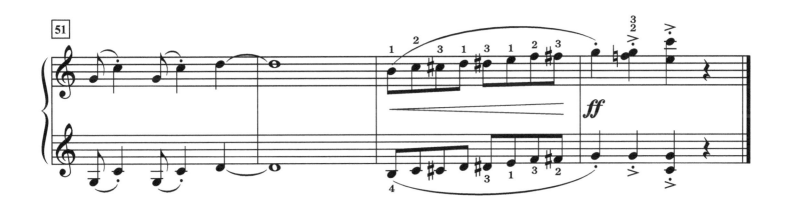

Minnesota Morning
SECONDO

Melody Bober

Minnesota Morning

PRIMO

Melody Bober

Flowing, peaceful (♩ = 80)
Play both hands one octave higher throughout

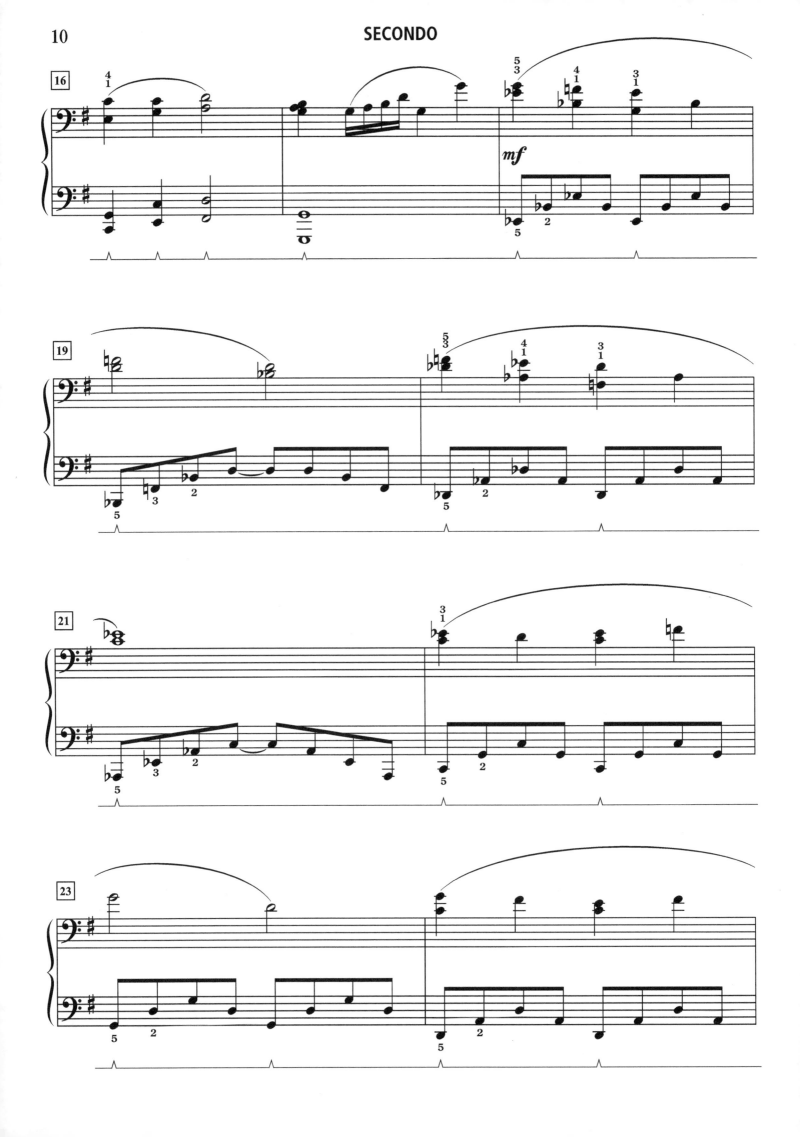

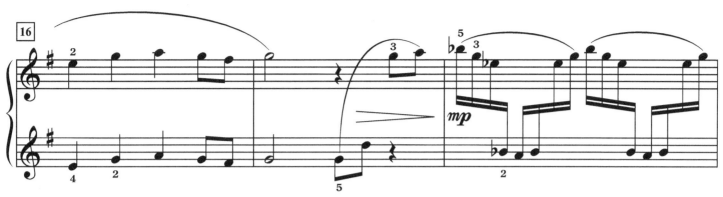

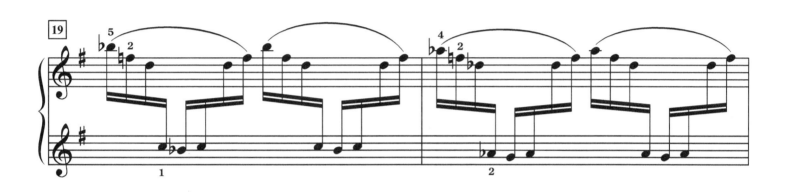

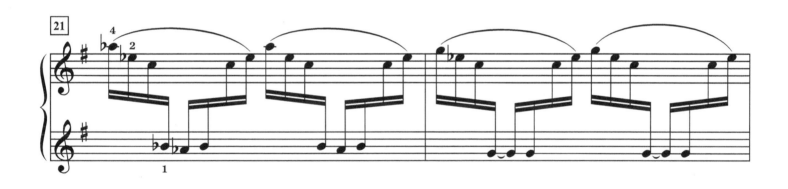

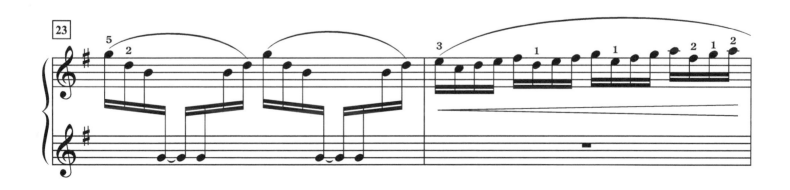

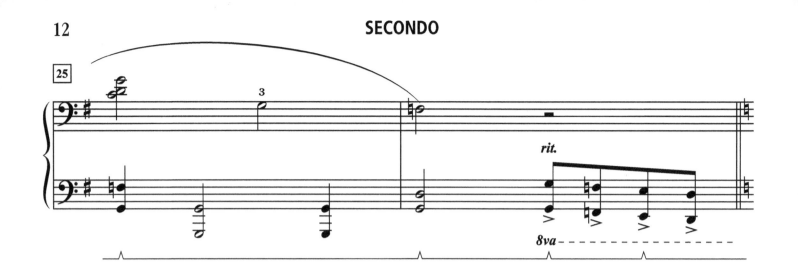

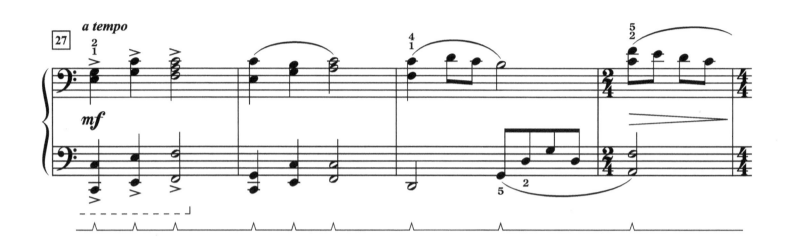

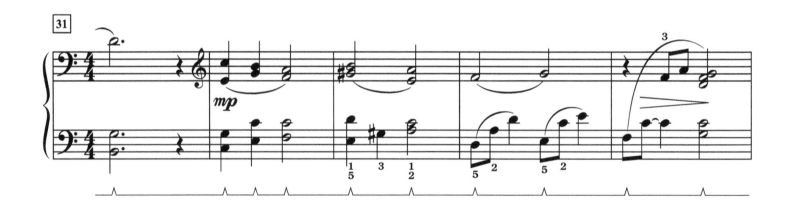

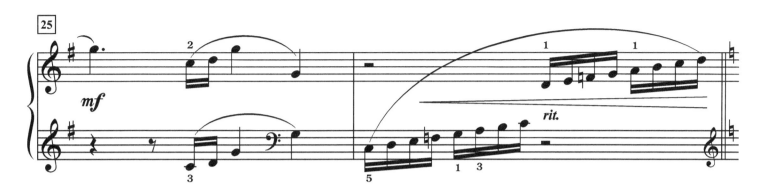

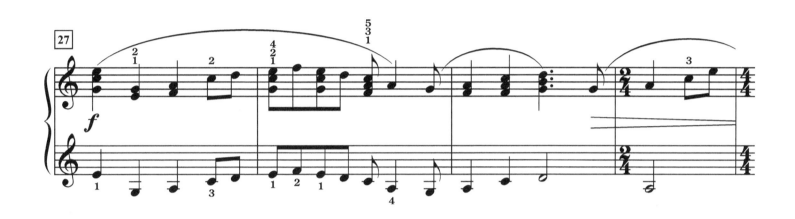

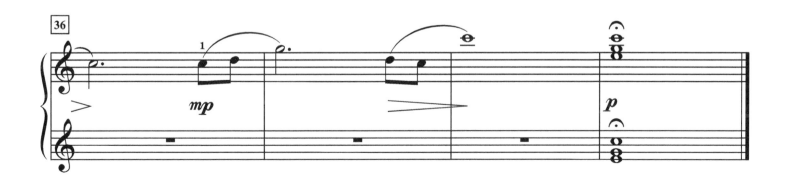

Blizzard
SECONDO

Melody Bober

Blizzard
PRIMO

Melody Bober

Forcefully (♩ = 108–112))
Play both hands one octave higher throughout

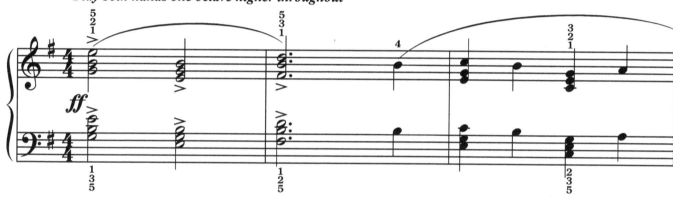

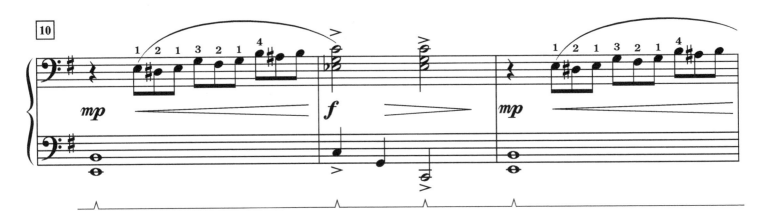

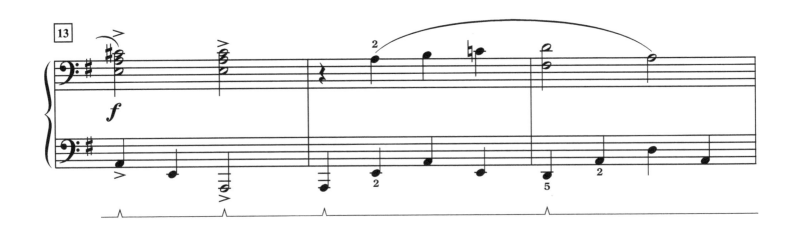

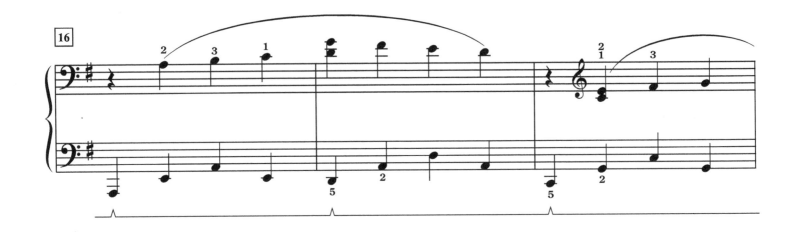

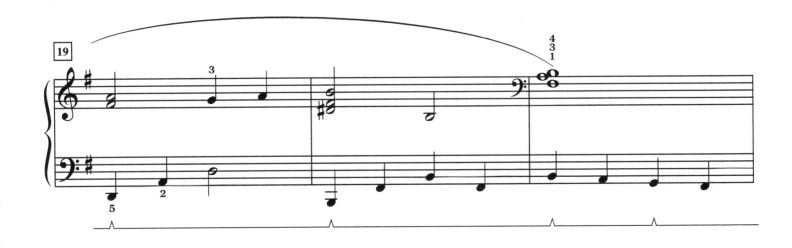

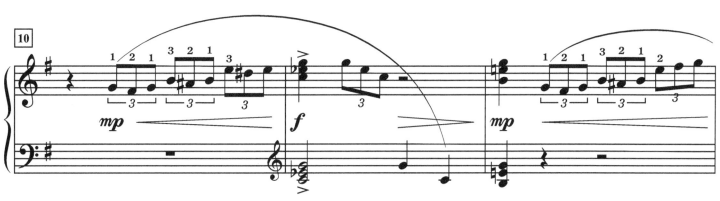

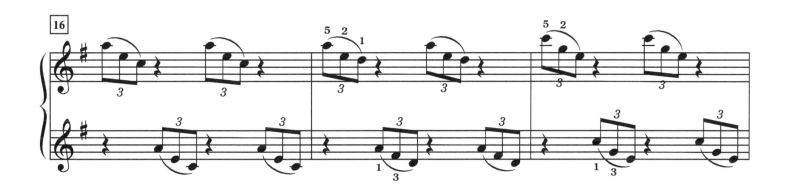

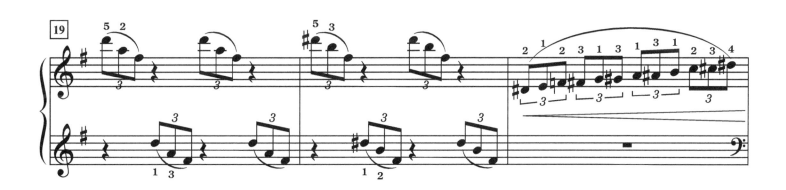

SECONDO

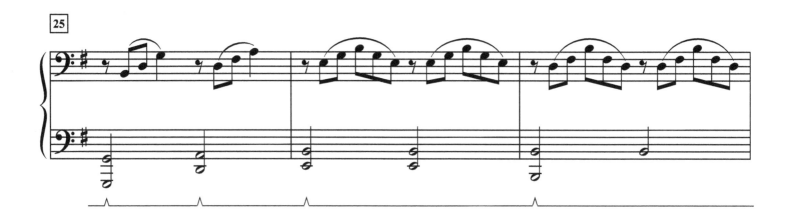

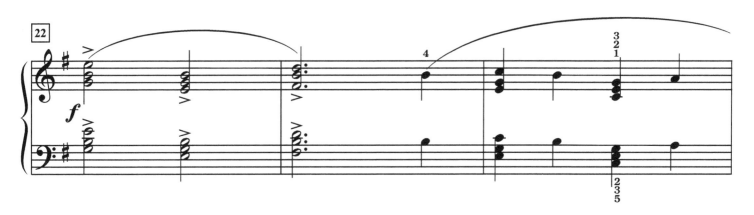

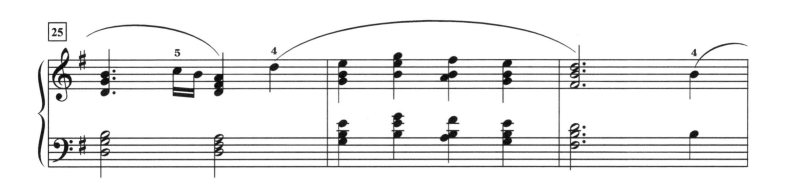

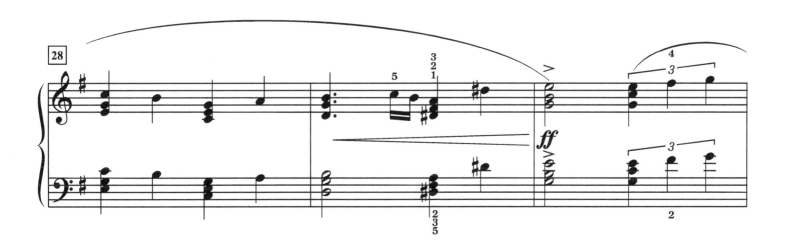

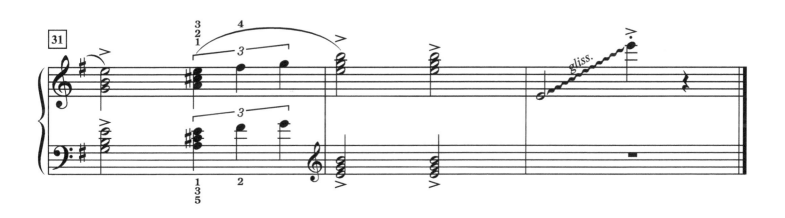